Timewise

Elisabeth Rowe

Oversteps Books

First published in 2019 by
Oversteps Books Ltd
6 Halwell House
South Pool
Nr Kingsbridge
Devon
TQ7 2RX
UK

www.overstepsbooks.com

Copyright © 2019 Elisabeth Rowe
ISBN 978-1-906856-84-7

All rights reserved. No part of this book may be reproduced, stored in a retrieval system, or transmitted in any form, or by any means, electronic, mechanical, photocopying, recording or otherwise, or translated into any language, without prior written permission from Oversteps Books, except by a reviewer who may quote brief passages in a review.

The right of Elisabeth Rowe to be identified as the author of this work has been asserted by her in accordance with the Copyright, Designs and Patents Act 1988.

Printed in Great Britain by imprint digital, Devon

For Dawn

Acknowledgements

Skin was long-listed in the Yeovil Literary Prize Writing Without Restrictions category 2018
The Berry Picker won 3rd prize in the Wells Festival of Literature Poetry Competition 2018
Dragonfly was short-listed in the Grey Hen Poetry Competition 2017
Priest's Cove was short-listed in the Wells Festival of Literature Poetry Competition 2018
Burning Gold and *No one Takes Photographs at Funerals* were both short-listed in the Wells Festival of Literature Poetry Competition 2013
Silk Road was long-listed in the Poetry on the Lake competition, 2015.

litel gold in cofre on page 34 is taken from Geoffrey Chaucer's description of the clerk in the Prologue to the Canterbury Tales.

Contents

The Col	1
The Wait	2
Snuff Box	3
Ocean Rift	4
Dancing Bear	5
Silk Road	6
Obsession	7
Thin Air	8
Acknowledgement	9
Too much Light	10
Wild Irises	11
What they did not tell me	12
Hair today	14
Skin	16
A Feather	18
Something, Nothing	19
The Berry Picker	20
Watch Tower	21
Winter Wisdom	22
Dragonfly	23
Priest's Cove	24
A Visitation	25
Gannets	26
Rapids	27
Time and again ...	28
Forest	30
Totem Poles	31
Letters from Udaipur	32
Burning Gold	34
Gold-sucker	35
Iron in the soil	36
The Scale of Things	37
Abbaye de Sénanque	38
Unknown	40
Mother Mine	41
The Valley	42

Running	43
Missing	44
Forgive me, Life	45
By the Way	46
No One Takes Photographs at Funerals	47
Creed	48
Doing Time	49
Night	50
When the World Ends	51

The Col

Ahead, the path surrenders
to the tilt and thrust of granite,
the prowling clouds.
Somewhere up there
a hut and the warm fug
of fellow travellers
cursing the treachery of bodies,
opening their hearts
as strangers will,
heady with relief
that they are not among
the missing.
Another level gained, but
here for the first time
I feel old.

Behind, the twist and plummet
of the track, the valley
patched in miniature
with green and gold.
Like the contrail overhead
my life streams backwards,
purposeful at first,
then dissipating in a shoal
of fluffy nothings.
Beneath my feet
a seething mass of magma
seeks a fault-line. The air
is thinning, the future
is a hard climb, and this
another false col.

The Wait

I need to know where the past is going.
I can't hold a thought for long,

nor remember the redemption
that once lived in a word,
a touch,
a leaf bending to rain.

Time flows backwards some days,
as a river may be a sea
sidling upstream –

spilling sky-silver on the mudflats,
swinging the line of boats
to face the ocean.

And so I wait,
patient as the heron,
for some meaning to come upon me,

some flotsam gift served up
on the creeping flood,

some glad tiding.

Snuff Box

I hold in my hand
   a little wooden shoe,
   my hand caressing
its silky history.
It no longer holds
   a copper sulphate crystal,
   the only treasure
I stole from science.
It holds the sound
   of my grandfather's stick
   tap-tapping the pavement,
the mushroomy smell
of his shiny scalp as
   we sat in his study
   by the hissing gas fire,
translating the letters of
Pliny the Younger;
   or waited fidgeting
   for breakfast oatcakes
bestowed as graciously
as golden sovereigns.

It's taken over sixty years
   for me to discover
   what the little keepsake
had once been used for,
long before holding
   the whispered secret
   that I might be grandfather's
favourite grandchild.
Last week I noticed
   on a stall in the market,
   among the collectibles,
two small wooden shoes
shiny and pointy-toed –
   snuff boxes, a fiver each!
   All change is for the worse,
my grandfather told me.
I didn't believe him.
   Only when we're old
   do we ask the questions
we should have asked the old
when we were young.

Ocean Rift

Why spend your time
snorkelling the warm seductive reefs
of recollection,

bright and busy with flicker
in the bend of light?

Why scurry surreptitiously
among those memories rooted
in shallow silt?

Strap on the air tank, mask and fins,
dive deep into those caverns where
the lumbering things you cannot name
roam their blind alleys.

Ignore the motes of panic dancing
in your torch beam,
discover in the rift a lost ecology
of remembrances.

Hang out with them, persuade them
to return with you,
pacing yourselves carefully
to avoid the bends,

then teach them gently how to share
the light.

Dancing Bear

At first it's exciting,
like kids signalling with mirrors
from hill to hill –

coming alive in the fierce shining of another,
the heart's gold rush;

but one day you may see returned to you
your own reflection,

a narrative of need not love,
all that grief and longing
a mere projection

and you exposed like a dancing bear
chained to a myth
of your own making.

How to love without binding,
that's the imperative:
not waiting

till your whole life sneaks up on you
ready to shout, *Bang! Bang!*
You're dead!

Silk Road

nightly
in the dark of the mind
your hands travel the silk road
of the body

moonlight splashes the mountains
washes the barren plains
silvers the pomegranate
cradled in thorns

you move lightly
resting to draw water
through parched lips
at each oasis

to bargain for sweet-meats
at each crossroad, honeyed
apricot and almond,
soft shawls the colour of blood
and bruise

always
you hear voices calling like birds
like water over stone

you know time lies in wait
for the ambush

wake to snow falling, ice
fashioning its spears
at the window

Obsession

Welcome the quiet days,
tide gentling over wrinkled sand,
the whole smiling sky in its lap.

Soon it comes plucking at kelp-frond,
nudging anemone, mussel, crab,
the suck and tug of small things
in the interstices,

building a long crescendo hammering of waves
to breathe salt music in the brooding
basalt cavern.

Reason sits throned on the shore
but holds no sway over the flood tide
of obsession.

Brace against sea's violence, its wind-whipped
hurling at hard edge, clash
of back-wash and inrush like
stallions rearing.

How to cling to the dizzying interface,
spray-hazed, seeded with thrift,
sung by the screaming birds?

Rock falls, land slips – nothing is safe
or solid as it seems in all this
lunge and lapse,

water and earth in a ceaseless dance
of attrition, each eager to re-make
and break the other.

Thin Air

We are resting side by side,
but you are somewhere far away
where the air is Himalaya-thin
in the labyrinth of your lungs.

Your words snatch and tug
like prayer flags in the wind;
no breath to spare for
murmured consolation.

Rope up, my friend, for the climb;
put one breath in front of another.
I'll be your Sherpa, shoulder your pack,
cut footsteps in the snow.

My eyes blur like melt-water;
yours are already fixed
on the icefalls ahead, the gully
and the impossible summit.

Acknowledgement

Impossible to look you in the eye or say
the words – your pain nudges mortality
up close and unambiguous.

Afraid to strip away the bark, lay bare
the raw fibre of your suffering,
I turn away, wanting

the unspeakable to be invisible
or leave discreetly, concealing
its reproaches.

When it's my turn, when in my unbelief
I pray for remission, tasking others
with the compassionate gaze,

the words of consolation to withstand
each dark unnerving raid
of the unthinkable,

will they look away, folding their origami
of denial, or will they offer some
simple affirmation,

acknowledging the hurt of our aloneness,
the ordinary unimagined mystery
of our shared being?

Too much Light

After we die, he told me,
when there was still time,

something of us returns
to universal consciousness.

It sounds like another version
of loneliness in a crowd:

how will our particles discover
one another in such flux?

I can't forgive his gift of light,
the long shadow of his leaving.

Let everything return to being
as it was: the candles lit,

the wine trembling in the glass,
time a ribbon of gold.

Wild Irises

I shall write about the irises,
how pluckily they hurl
their acid spears
into the back of winter.

I wish that I could stay
until the late spring sunshine
melts the irises to pools
of gaudy yellow

and return, at summer's end,
to pick a sheaf of pale papery leaves
and weave a little basket
for remembrance.

What they did not tell me

They did not warn me
in all their kindly professional sessions,
eye to eye with the bad news,
that I would lose part of my self along with
a breast and all my hair.

I got used to the monotony of corridors,
sucked into the slip-stream of the sick,
the damaged and the dying;

but not to the swift shift of emphasis,
that renders the invalid somehow in-valid,
down-grades agent to patient, active to passive,
exposed to the multiple laying on of hands,
subject to the linguistic hegemony
of drugs, prostheses and technologies,
the lazy metaphors of battle and survival.

I got used to the stranger in the mirror,
her face sharp as an axe, thighs like sticks,
skin blotched or barnacled,
head naked as a stone –
but not to the absent self, the familiar friend
whose outside matched the inside,
who smiled back at me and told me
I could go about the world
with confidence.

A good prognosis, they tell me, reassuringly:
but everyone knows pathology plays hide and seek,
and patients learn to make good eye contact
with mortality.

Spread-eagled on the scanner bed
in my single-breasted birthday suit,
focussing on the radiographer's quiff
of peacock blue hair as he maps
and marks my body, I feel
a curious rush of love for all who do this work.
I thank them for their compassion,
their skill in making matter-of-fact the stuff
of human suffering –

but they did not warn me how extensively
the house of my being would be rubbled,
or tell me how it shall be re-built.

Hair today ....

Hair today, gone tomorrow
is a genuine sorrow.

It may seem like an insignificant calamity,
an unworthy display of vanity,

but a head of hair in both quality and quantity
affirms one's identity!

So let's have no more jolly jokery
about wiggery-pokery;

don't talk about bald-head tattoos
to those who have nothing hairy to lose;

don't suggest a new look, purple perhaps –
it might cause a relapse!

The long and the short of it is: loved or hated,
my hair and I have always been closely related.

It always seemed instinctively to know why
I needed a cut and blow dry,

so when the last duck-fluff is no longer standing on end
it's like the death of an old friend.

And what am I supposed to do
with all those reproachful bottles of shampoo?

People tell me it will soon grow again
but who knows when?

Teasing me that it might come back curly
is guaranteed to make me surly.

Find me something awesome to compensate
for my uninvited hairless pate –

there's not a lot of laughs
in all those arty bandannas and scarfs.

One thing to put my mind at rest:
several birds have probably lined the nest

with comb-fuls of fugitive hair
thrown to the four winds in despair.

Skin

skin
      is what we arrive
and leave
      in
         whatever colour skin
you are born within
        black or white or something
    in between
skin
  from baby-nuzzly
      to bark-wrinkly   is designed
    to be lived in
skin
    keeps you in
        even though you may be fat
and it is thin
     skin
        keeps on stretching
            with each year etching
the lines of time
        skin
    is something we are exhorted
  to be
        comfortable in
            but sometimes
it goes awry, supplies
        a hotchpotch
  of spots and blotches
          suddenly
with no apology
      a dermatological
    cosmology
        skin
    betrays the mood you're in
that blush that flush
        of adrenaline

skin
        conceals the person within
        yours may be thick
                and mine thin
     skin
   the sweet-wrapper wherein
we hide each impulse to goodness
         each committed sin
    skin
       is where we begin
and end
     make it your friend

A Feather

They call us the survivors,

persuade us to collude with metaphors
of strife and overcoming

that cast remission as a victory
of our own making,

bright with the prospect of a
permanent peace –

as though we have been given
a new body, a new life, not the old one
re-visited

with the old skirmishes,
the old illusions and a new burden
of gratefulness.

There is no lasting truce.
Light returns, and shade
its faithful follower.

We are not heroic, merely hungry
for safety,

knowing survival is a feather
on a breath.

Something, Nothing

Something flew into my heart,
arrowed like a contrail
into my blue centre.
The birds were absent,
the sky was resting on the lake,
a still ambivalence
of air and water.
It was no more than the shadow of a crane
moving on the surface,
the shiver of a leaf in the alders
ahead of the wind,
but I knew it for that part of myself
that had gone missing.
It weighed almost nothing
in the palm of my heart
but I felt a quickening, urgent
as the harsh crawk of the crane,
and I took it for a restoration,
a shift away from loss,
a flow of light.

***

We came to the sea for the birds –
geese flying south for days, they said,
but the sky was silent.
We picked a way
through a twist of pine and birch
to the great bleached slabs of granite
with their silky fringe of weed
where the sea had sunk.
Beyond the lighthouse
white sails blew in and out of sight;
a cormorant flapped from east to west;
inshore a dragonfly half as big as a bird
patrolled the rocks.
Later that day perhaps or the next
a million migrant geese would darken the sky
with their winged urgency, but
such visitations come at times
of their own choosing, so we turned away
and the forest swallowed us
and all our longing.

The Berry Picker

A slight re-alignment of light and shade
and she's there, solid as a tree
in this place of trees,

held in a column of sunlight,

a concentrated presence
emerging from the forest in the fullness
of belonging.

Cushioned in blueberry scrub
the child at her feet is combing the bushes
with a metal scoop, tumbling the fruits
into her birch-bark basket.

Swathed and scarfed against bug-bite
and crab-fly scurry, the woman tilts her head
to a shifting sky;

to a glint of lake beyond the trees,
where light joins and divides like pools
of mercury.

Change on the wind, rain coming,
the long-limbed pines sky-sighing.

She stretches, bunching her fists to her back,
then bends to take the harvest from
the child with indigo lips.

A sudden swift cloud-shadow
and they are gone, vanishing into
a chequered colonnade,

their after-image vivid as a waking dream

while overhead cranes head north,
like raucous oracles declaring,
'Winter will come.'

Watch Tower

We are heading north
for the midnight sun,
nothing but uniform
grey-green trees
and a long arm of road
nudging the border.

We are scanning
the middle distance
for the first watch tower,
expecting some
shock of recoil from
its alien glamour,

but it's a crude affair –
a spindly pylon frame
half hidden in spruce
with a platform and
some tiny men watching us
watching them.

This is Karelia
stolen land of music
memory and death;
its exiles know the forest
will outstrip soviet towers
and all they stand for.

Borders are fragile,
temporary cases of
this side and that side
as history is before
and after, but right now
we are heading north,

wrapped in our own
taken-for-granted freedoms.
Soon we shall be
scanning willow scrub
for the first reindeer,
the first cloudberry.

Winter Wisdom

Write your winter wisdom
when the words run dry,
you told me.

What do you expect?
Some kind of silver weathered word-flow,
life-bytes of a linguistic surfer?

I'm telling you, that stuff
is for the birds, who, if they have any sense,
have flown to somewhere warm.

All I have to offer is a grey head-space
obliging with bad habits, blotched capacities,
bent expectations.

Old age is the punishment
for growing old.
No spring greens for the body,
no hey nonny-no
the lover and his lass long gone.

Leaf-fall turns to loam and feeds the roots
that shoot to light and air,
but don't you see how all renewal
is reserved for youth?

Winter wisdom is the past set solid,
the future below ground,
the present splintered
with survival.

Feed it to the birds, and ask me
about summer
while I can still remember it.

Dragonfly

You skim the sky-in-water
with such dazzling aerobatic ease

it's hard to imagine your *mafioso* days
in the murky under-world,

awaiting the summons, the paling,
the pull of light

that taught you how to drag your body
up an anchored reed

towards the sudden ravishing of air –
the first breath.

Hard to believe in transformation:

warmth splitting the skin behind your head,
fracturing your larval carapace,

unfolding the lacework of your see-through wings
for the miracle of flight.

Priest's Cove

A black gash of ancient moon-rock
salt-slick and sombre;

no sea-suck and swell, a tongue
of light scarcely licking
the slipway.

One seal beyond the kelp-beds
surfaces, sinks, surfaces,
keeping an eye.

Beyond banks of speckled stones
tide-rolled and polished
by time

my children and their children
are combing wet pebbles
for specks of glass,

junk bottles ground into jewels,
sneaking the sun – green,
amber, sapphire.

Over and over ocean proves itself
king and keeper, revealing,
concealing, revealing

while each generation grows
into its own sense of rock
and belonging.

A Visitation

The kestrel came to her,
eye to eye level,

hung on the up-draught working the air
between granite and spume,

a scoop of sandy cliff his whole intention.

She saw the white flecks on his breast,
his orange feet tucked close

before he plunged.

She waited, hopeful,

while little flocks of sea-foam
skittered overhead.

Gannets

These are his first gannets.
Some trick of wind and tide
has drawn them to a festival of fish –
fifty, a hundred, white-flecking
the oyster sea,

rising in turn to circle, scanning
the surface for a hint of silver,
each sudden plummeting
a marvel of feathered
weaponry.

He marks their precision,
the sequin squirm of fish in the skirmish,
the great birds surfacing, swallowing,
shaking their black-tipped wings
for the take-off

until a fishing boat,
running to Padstow before tide-turn,
bisects their feeding ground,
lifting the flotsam congregation
in a slow snow-flurry.

Inshore, three seals watch the boy
head back along the cliff,
turning and turning,
the distance darkening between him
and his homing point, the gannets
swallowed in the dying light
as sunset bloodies the bay.

Rapids

remember
that day on Snake River

the Colorado sun
slung heavy
the river sheened as glass

the glass buckling
the boat plunging into rough

bucking the crazy crests
smacking the hollows

the whole river
gathering itself
and heading for the cliff

someone screaming
Lean in! Lean in!

as the flimsy rib
slams into rock
ricochets

twists away
down a long chute
of chastened water

they called it *Oh Shit Rock*
but we had yet to learn
how there is always

something lying in wait
to trouble the natural flow
of things

Time and again ...
For Nikki van Schyndel of Echo Bay

I am here, now,
crouched on a nameless rock in the Pacific
pulling wild onions from a cache of salty soil,
stripping them to the white and sniffing mint for
a survivalist stir-fry;

and now here,
thrashing a trail through head-high tangles of blackberry
and thimbleberry to the massive doorway frame
of a ruined tribal *bighouse*, and a fallen totem
rotting in the undergrowth.

I am here, now,
crunching a beach thick-layered with ancient clamshells,
where a line of stubby posts is all that survives
of the missionaries with their godly intentions
and devilish legacy;

and now here,
sitting by a camp fire eating the wilderness foragings
from clamshell bowls and mussel spoons, sheltered
beneath giant cedars draped with wispy lichen
like fading prayer flags.

Watch me now
willing myself to be present here for ever,
practising this Being in the Moment thing
with all the intensity I can muster, though I am
already grieving.

Could it be
that everything is actually happening at once;
that some neurological anomaly, some god-trick
or space-time warp conspires to create
our linear illusion?

I am here, now,
sitting at home in a wooded Dartmoor valley
watching the drizzle bead unruly flower-heads,
plastic-wrapped supermarket salmon fridged
for an un-earned supper.

Everything aches
to be back in the islands, sharing the moods of ocean
with orca and eagle, salmon and dolphin, where rest
is a boat at anchor, and time nothing but
a gigantic hoax.

Forest

Some do not even look –

their journey is arrival
not discovery, forest means nothingness
and inconvenience.

Others look but do not see
beyond undifferentiated
greenness

to register the whole sweet breathing mass of it,
its singular fullness.

Count me among the ones who look and see
forest in its plurality –

a mighty collective,
each tree struggling to assert
its claim on light and air;

each one a precious variation on
the theme of tree, a miracle
of improvisation;

how each branch is home and host
to bird and beetle, lichen
and parasite,

how each twig holds raindrops
budding like beads of light.

Forgive me when I harry you
to look and look again, to see
the truth of forest:

a living metaphor for birth and death
and restoration.

Totem Poles

In the time before we came to silence them
with missionary zeal and mortal sickness
the Haida lived on the edge,
knew only what sun and moon and wind
and tide revealed to them:

how spirit moves through all things, how little
separates man from raven, eagle, salmon
or killer whale; how one becomes another
in their mythology of transformation.

These are their mortuary poles,
bleached grey, leaning like old men
at the edge of a crescent bay,
the carved features of beaver, bear and dogfish
scarred by rain and time,
the pinnacled coffin-boxes sprouting ferns.

They will rot and fall,
surrender their story to the forest floor
from which they grew in monumental groves
of cedar, spruce and hemlock.
Everything here is busy being born
or dying, growth and decay the seamless
order of things.

At the Haida heritage centre,
a new pole lies in the womb of the carving shed.
Hundreds gather to bear witness to its birth
and help deliver it to the weathering elements
on its way to a sacred site.

They hold their past in the palm of the present,
to keep tradition alive, to remind us
that the earth does not belong to us,
we belong to the earth:
looking and seeing how everything is connected,
we may choose to be care-takers
or destroyers.

Haida Gwaii, formerly known as the Queen Charlotte Islands and home to the Haida people, is an archipelago c.130 miles west of Prince Rupert in British Columbia

Letters from Udaipur

Taken from letters from my grandfather in India to my father at school in England

Camp, Udaipur. Touring a wonderful country,
my head full of a Greek translation of Tennyson's
Crossing the Bar.
My camel was man-handled down a precipice,
coaxed by my camel man's volleys of endearments:
Proceeding with extreme caution, my pearl –
the she-camels await thee at the bottom!

Your school report is excellent and exhilarating.

Glad you are making way in mathematics –
the nearest thing to absolute truth available to our minds.
The making of beautiful things a part of oneself
is a fine thing. Read Plotinus
on the spiritual vision above and beyond reason.
It is got by prayer and thinking on things that are true,
honest, pure, just and of good report.

Ideas are the life of every civilisation.

Yesterday went shooting for my Christmas dinner:
two red-headed pochard, a spot-billed duck, a partridge
and nine snipe. Nothing to do in the evenings here
but stroll out with a gun. One gets tired of the eternal tennis.
I have been watching paradise fly-catchers build their cobweb nest –
I always think birds are about the most beautiful creatures
or *thoughts* of the creative spirit.

Have the tree-creepers come back to the redwood tree?

Congress has voted for complete severance from the Empire –
there are proposals for civil disobedience.
Little prospect now of Indian service for Englishmen:
young men will go to Canada to farm musk-oxen.

I shall not be able to give you a shilling of capital.

I attended a *durbar*, perhaps the last for His Highness:
a beautiful sunset spectacle in the palace courtyard,
gold pinnacles and prancing caparisoned horses.
HH frail but dignified in pink satin, wearing his emeralds,
his nobles silent, watching with wolfish faces.
For forty years he has held them down with an iron hand.

Don't buy a tail coat yet, as my tailor will make you one.

The city is dark and filthy, riddled with disease:
thousands of children died last year of small-pox.
HH will have no water supply within the walls,
yet his court is the wonder and delight of the Indian world.
Congress has told the rulers of the Indian States
they are a disgrace to their country and must pass into the night.

God save us from a beneficent despot!

A narrowly avoided tragedy today:
my dog Peter came nose to nose with a Russell's viper,
deadliest of snakes. You take two days to die,
bleeding through the skin. On this cheerful note I will end.
Much love to you. If you are hard up, tell your mother:
there's still a shot in the locker. Your loving father.

Burning Gold

And did those feet in ancient times
walk in Kolkata's fetid alleyways?
Find me a poet-priest to hymn this legend,
take him to the fabled goldsmiths' quarter
where gilded women glide,
insured with treasure chains around their necks
and arms and ankles;
show him the narrow passage paved with glitter
shaken from the craftsmen's hair,
washed from their skins, dispersed like ancient stars
in the blackness of street filth and sewer slurry;
let him watch the man who rises before dawn
to gather truant particles of glister
finer than dead skin dust;
who sweeps the gutter dirt and pans it
hour by choking hour for infinitesimal
specks of hope; or worse,
the man immersed neck-deep in a city drain,
who hauls up sacks of stinking sludge
and loads his chariots of filth to sell
to another band of panners.
Teach him their arcane alchemy,
the drying, sieving, beating, smelting,
all for a *litel gold in cofre*, weighed
and sold back to the goldsmiths.
Will the poet-prophet, sword in hand, reflect
a small redemptive light in this other
dark satanic cycle,
where clouds unfold over the sacred Ganges?
Each fires his arrows of desire, each dreams
his own advancement and a modest gleam
of wealth a few rungs up the leaden ladder,
a few miles down the golden road;
each builds his own version of Jerusalem
with wits and courage, daring to exploit
what others fail to see,
the gold that's hidden in the garbage
of their lives.

Gold-sucker

What's new?

A eucalyptus tree sucks gold
from thirty metres down –
the tree is thirsty, roots mine deep,
discover water and deliver it
by trunk and branch roads to the veins of leaves;
the gold just hitches a ride.

Gold leaf occurring naturally – what's new?
Nature creates the jazziest installations.
Someone will soon be seeking to exploit
the tree's divining power,
the lucre-lyptus lustre of those silvery leaves
that host the golden dust.

No gum tree gold rush, though –
the precious metal's eighty parts per billion.
No desperate prospectors rolling in
with their dusty wagons and exhausted women
to pan the fallen leaves, no outback surgeons
tapping the peeling trunks for golden syrup,
no modern phyto-mining engineers –

just the odd adventurer with an eye
for the needs of those who already have everything.

What's new?

We are all sap-suckers in our way,
harvesting nano-particles of gilt
from the deep strata of our disaffection.

I say to the eucalyptus *you are beautiful,*
your silver spinners flashing in the fierce
Antipodean noon, your whispering canopy
lit by the abracadabra hand of night
beneath the Southern Cross:

you need no further testament.

Iron in the soil

We're playing follow-my-leader to the menhir
a sheepish rag-bag of amateurs
booted and Gore-Texed for the Dartmoor drizzle,
aiming our two bent wire coat-hangers
like alien antennae.

The makeshift rods swing inwards,
crossing in sympathy, our mentor says,
with the energy beneath:
mist and a mellow moorland mysticism
conspire to suspend our disbelief.

Snug in a self-fulfilling prophecy,
we greet the granite giant with a hug.
We're thinking force fields, ley lines,
some kind of magnetism, iron in the soil,
perhaps. No one cracks a smile.

Aligned with two stone avenues
flanking a sluggish leat, the rods grow urgent,
as though fine-tuned to an ancient tug –
earth-energy travelling east up one row,
west down the other.

We're talking biosensors now,
connections to our inner wisdom. Call it
credulity, confirmation bias, what you will,
we watch the humble wire coat-hanger
confounding science.

No evidence *de mysteria* will prevail
against the scoffing sceptic, but this day
nothing can douse the magic of the rods'
autonomous response, their irreducible
seductive twitch.

The Scale of Things

Here we could reach out and touch a thousand
fireflies pulsing in the olive trees,
while thirty miles away, streak lightning tears
the sky to shreds above the Apuan alps.

Sometimes our energy will harness itself
to wrong events – a tale told once too often,
a wailing infant, an abandoned sock –
unleashing a bolt of pure malevolence.

When the storm grumbles away to nothing,
fireworks are over, and the darkness thickens,
there lingers in the stifling air a sense
of violation in the scale of things.

Hornets are feasting in the almond tree.
We could reach out and touch a million stars.

Abbaye de Sénanque

Here they come, massing from the coach park.
Signs scream *Silence!* but the guide
must talk his tour group loudly
through eight centuries of sanctuary.

> *prayer-tranced and feverish*
> *with lack of sleep, he stumbles*
> *into the cool colonnades blinking*
> *at the plain ecstasy of day*

Dodge into the cloisters, space for meditation
and soul's nourishment; but here they come,
clacking down the steps, un-chastened,
clustering and craning for the bell tower.

> *look how the garden's stern geometry*
> *invites austere restraint:*
> *orderly box hedge, scented myrtle*
> *schooled to obedience*

Escape into the church, its Romanesque austerity
profoundly peaceable. But here they come,
glazed faces searching for a point of reference,
already surfeiting on stifling sanctity.

> *every night and morning of his life*
> *these stones are witness to the rhythm*
> *of his body's needs, his soul's struggle,*
> *the secrets of his heart*

And there they go, ticking off chapter house,
refectory, shop. The buses leave. Now silently
return to the dormitory, lie on the cold stone floor,
let your eyes wander the gloomy ceiling vaults.

and when the birds have flown home
and perhaps the angels also,
he gazes at the arched blue canopy
of heaven with sudden anguish

Then go out into the merciless sunlight
to the lavender fields, row upon row
blanketing the hillside like a habit,
and blink away eight hundred years.

Unknown

I have been so long coming
to this place

I no longer recognise
the landscape of my body –

the shift and schist of its relentless
metamorphosis –

this waterscape of mind
sullen and tremulous
beneath the pull of moons.

I say to my reflection,
Welcome, stranger,

and it looks back at me
as strangers do,

unfocussed, making no
concessions.

Mother Mine

I scarcely noticed you at first:
you were nothing but a prickling
in my upper lip, a tweak
at the corners of my mouth.
But when you twitched my nostrils,
pursed my lips and sniffed a judgment
small but irredeemable,
I knew you had moved in.

Now you are everywhere,
travelling my blood stream
like a parasite,
seeking the tender places,
making yourself at home.
You hunch my shoulders,
square the nails on my useful hands
and ink the tributary veins
behind my knees.

Mother mine, it's not easy to say
you're not welcome here:
I have obligations, I acknowledge
the many comforts and affirmations
of mothers, but listen,
we are not sitting comfortably together
in this body of mine.

Day by day I feel my bones
grumbling and thinning, my back
curving and shrinking
with the weight of you; exhausted,
bruised, I long for respite.
Where can I make my refuge,
where else can I hide
but in my daughter?

The Valley

It's been there all along,
the valley of the shadow,
while I busied myself among the hills.

There's always been a mist
in the valley of the shadow
but I've been basking on sunlit summits.

Now that my hips and knees are aching
and my head is no longer good for heights
I'm spending time on the lower slopes,

where the mist is closing tight about me
in the valley of the shadow.
My feet are icy cold

and my heart is afraid
as I follow down the stony track
in the valley of the shadow.

Running

you are running, running

no whence or whither, only a needled path
beneath the watching trees

look

the forest is spread with sweet wild strawberries
kneel and taste

listen

a bird is whistling, summoning blue-black night

don't be afraid of the darkening sky
the mutterings of the forest

look up

all night long the stars run leaping and laughing
over the sky

but in your dream

the beast of the forest paws you to death
on a bed of wild strawberries

the bird spreads its ragged black wing-span
over your bones

the stars rattle your soul in their sieve

and you are falling, falling

down to the soft thick forest floor where

you start running, running

Missing

It just upped and offed without any warning
like a sparrowhawk, secretive, swerving low.
I might have guessed it would be disillusioned,
restive after our many years together:

I broke my promise to take it somewhere exotic –
an ice hotel, a tropical reef, a pyramid.
I should have exposed it to volcano rims,
black ski runs, hurricanes, something extreme.

It must have given me up for a bad job
and taken a gap year to fulfil itSelf.
Without it I am insubstantial, lack-lustre.
I want to say, *come back, all is forgiven!*

Will someone kindly put out an SOS
on the wireless, next to the six o'clock pips:

This is a message for Self:
Last seen going about its business in the usual way,
believed to be travelling abroad and incognito.
Please contact your owner who is dangerously diminished
or call Scotland Yard on Whitehall 1212

Forgive me, Life

for I have not sinned enough.
I came from a place of small transgressions:
even if I'd known there was a line to cross
I'd have been waiting at the gates while
temptation thundered past.
(I smoked a fag once on a family holiday –
my mother sniffed me out).

I never could let go.
Others head down the black run,
spur towards the triple jump, and test
their weight against the wind;
but gravity and speed are my sworn enemies,
and I'm a lifelong expert at falling short.
Loving is the one thing I do fearlessly:
I can love straight down the fall line,
clean over the water jump, and round
the Fastnet Rock.

I put my faith in another Life,
reserved for those whose inhibitions bind
their feet in this one:
there will be enough steam let off there
to power the universe.
Free-range passions,
love fairly traded and organic,
guilt-free flights of imagination.

Give me another chance, Life.

By the Way

You look like death, I say. He seems
pleased to be recognised,

and when I tell him I'm not quite ready
he shrugs and says, *I'll wait.*

In the garden his footprints scorch
the lawn like frost,

his breath dead-heads my late roses,
puts the swallows to flight.

I ponder my forwarding address, decide
there is time for a note:

*Just off. Remember to put the rubbish out,
and by the way ....*

No One Takes Photographs at Funerals

They hardly notice him, this
black-cassocked master of disposal,
there when the furnace doors glide open
to embrace the coffin – ashes to ashes –
there in the graveyard with the huddled mourners –
dust to dust. Death is a production line
like any other.

He never sees the body: he must
bring the dead to life with tear-stained scraps
furnished by the left-behind,
the so-called loved-ones longing to collude
in sure and certain hope.
After the resonant consoling words
most will return to the comfort
of unknowing.

Hard to go on affirming each botched body
has sloughed a soul that wings its way to heaven.
All this man knows for certain
is that death sifts our particles into a bowl
of new beginnings: someone is needed
to solemnise their passage, to be
their dark angel of the threshold,
the instrument of faith, the model
of compassion.

But being on intimate terms with our mortality
is costly to the spirit. All this machinery
serves to remind him that his own life-space
is shrinking towards oblivion –
earth to earth.
Someone should tell him not to neglect the living:
to stop, look and listen, take time to smile
at babies in prams, notice early snowdrops
in the cemetery, feel the quickening
of long-buried hope.

Creed

the words unfurl
take shape like candle smoke
curling among the dust motes

>   *the remission of sins*
>   *the resurrection of the dead*
>   *the life of the world to come*

make-believe affirmations
in the lovely long-ago language
that consoles and terrifies

if God is here

he is not wedged between worn pews
webbed in the stone roof ribs
or bleeding in a stained-glass window

>   God is here because I am here

and I am here because I cannot bring myself
to say I believe in nothing

beyond smoke and dust.

Doing Time

they call it doing time

an inept transitive
for time's intransigence
for the time being

it's not like
doing homework, yoga
or embroidery

more like nothing
dressed up in minutes
hours and days

doing time means time
marking time, tock-ticking
all the way to nowhere

outside they do time
differently

they do the school run
jobs or gym

they do the lawn, the laundry
killer sudoku

only inside are they
doing time

a monk does time, but time
of his own choosing

not impossible perhaps

in the monkish sphere
of the un-chosen cell

to be doing time with
good intention

knowing time does for us all
in the end

Night

Moon muscles towards the full
One star burns ahead of the pack
Sky draws tight as a balaclava

A cow bellows for its taken calf
Owls scythe the secretive trees
Night as harsh as it gets in the valley

Sheltered from the elsewhere darkening
That shrouds our failure to redeem
The human project, or re-kindle hope

And freedom for the dispossessed
I think of our return to nothingness
Not as some kind of going into the dark

But a streaming of the fractured rainbows
Of our lives back through the prism
To be annihilated in white light

When the World Ends

When the world ends
The blind do not see the blinding flash
The deaf do not hear the deafening roar
The dumb give no warning to the lame
Who cannot run away
The madman laughs and claps his hands
The little child sits on the sand
And draws another circle

Oversteps Books Ltd

The Oversteps list includes books by the following poets:

David Grubb, Giles Goodland, Alex Smith, Will Daunt, Patricia Bishop, Christopher Cook, Jan Farquarson, Charles Hadfield, Mandy Pannett, Doris Hulme, James Cole, Helen Kitson, Bill Headdon, Avril Bruton, Marianne Larsen, Anne Lewis-Smith, Mary Maher, Genista Lewes, Miriam Darlington, Anne Born, Glen Phillips, Rebecca Gethin, W H Petty, Melanie Penycate, Andrew Nightingale, Caroline Carver, John Stuart, Rose Cook, Jenny Hope, Anne Stewart, Oz Hardwick, Terry Gifford, Michael Swan, Maggie Butt, Anthony Watts, Robert Stein, Graham High, Ross Cogan, Ann Kelley, Diane Tang, R V Bailey, John Daniel, Alwyn Marriage, Kathleen Kummer, Jean Atkin, Charles Bennett, Elisabeth Rowe, Marie Marshall, Ken Head, Robert Cole, Cora Greenhill, John Torrance, Michael Bayley, Christopher North, Simon Richey, Lynn Roberts, Sue Davies, Mark Totterdell, Michael Thomas, Ann Segrave, Helen Overell, Rose Flint, Denise Bennett, James Turner, Sue Boyle, Jane Spiro, Jennie Osborne, John Daniel, Janet Loverseed, Wendy Klein, Sally Festing, Angela Stoner, Simon Williams, Susan Taylor, Richard Skinner, Fokkina McDonnell, Joan McGavin, David Broadbridge, Sue Proffitt, Christine Whittemore, A C Clarke, Ian Royce Chamberlain, Melanie Branton, Denise McSheehy, Rebecca Bilkau, Jane Spiro, Hilary Elfick, Paul Surman, Antony Mair, Carol DeVaughn, Jenny Hockey and Patricia Leighton.

For details of all these books, information about Oversteps and up-to-date news, please look at our website and blog:

www.overstepsbooks.com
http://overstepsbooks.wordpress.com